NATURE Kids
The Kea

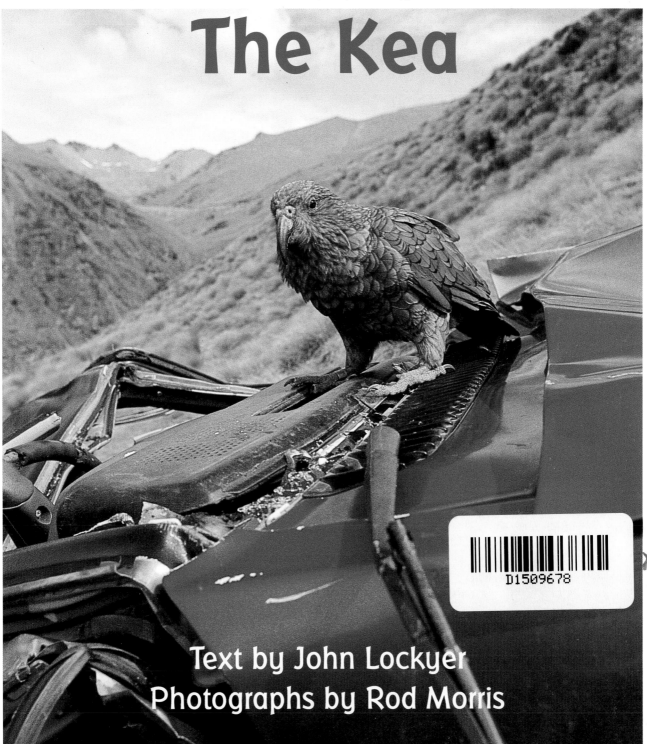

Text by John Lockyer
Photographs by Rod Morris

Established in 1907, Reed Publishing (NZ) Ltd
is New Zealand's largest book publisher, with over 300 titles in print.

For details on all these books visit our website:
www.reed.co.nz

Published by Reed Children's Books, an imprint of
Reed Publishing (NZ) Ltd, 39 Rawene Road, Birkenhead,
Auckland. Associated companies, branches and
representatives throughout the world.

ISBN 1 86948 877 6
First published 2001

Edited by Carolyn Lagahetau
Designed by Sharon Whitaker

Printed in New Zealand

Contents

Who, what, where?

Kea are mountain birds.
They live in New Zealand.
Kea are curious, playful and intelligent.
They are called the 'clowns of the mountains'.

Kea are not scared of people.

Kea will slide down roofs, play with balls, throw stones and steal anything left around.

Kea can be pests. They often rip and slash the rubber on bikes and cars.

Kea are scavengers.

Family tree

 There are about 10,000 kea in New Zealand.

Kea belong to the parrot family.
They are found only in the South Island of New Zealand.
They build their nests in the forests and fields of the high country.

Kea are not endangered but they are protected.

Kea are the only parrots that live in the mountains.

Male kea
can weigh up
to 1.2 kilograms.

Good looks

Male kea are larger than females.
Kea have sharp, curved bills.
They have strong feet with long claws.
Adult kea have green on the outside of
their wings and yellow on the underside.

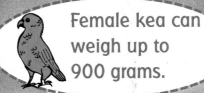

Female kea can weigh up to 900 grams.

Seeking and tasting

Kea look for food in forests and on rocky hillsides.
They will travel up to 10 kilometres from home to find food.
They choose their food by size, shape and colour.
Kea always taste their food with their tongues before eating it.

Kea feed early and late in the day.

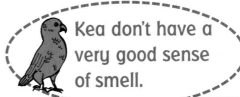

Kea don't have a very good sense of smell.

Kea use their bills to grip, rip and dig.

Dinnertime!

Kea break open live and rotten wood
to find insects, grubs and worms.
They turn over stones to eat roots,
seeds and leaves.
They suck nectar from flowers.

Kea will steal food off picnic tables.

On the skifields, kea eat food left by people.

Some kea will attack and feed on live sheep.

Sounds

Kea have many noisy, tuneless calls.
They screech when they fly.
When they are looking for a mate
or a neighbour, they warble.
The call kea make the most sounds
just like their name – 'kee-a'.

Kea give a warning cry when danger is near.

Home, sweet home

Kea use the same nest every year.

Kea make their nests between large rocks or in the hollows and roots of old trees. Their nests are hidden at the end of a long tunnel.
Female kea build the nests using dried moss, ferns, leaves and rotten wood.

Eggs

Female kea lay up to four eggs.

They sit on the eggs to keep them warm.

After 3 weeks, the chicks hatch.

They stay in the nest with their mother for 13 weeks.

During this time, male kea look for food to feed their new family.

A kea egg is half the size of a hen's egg.

Before new eggs are laid, nests are cleaned out and made again.

Kea eggs are laid between July and January.

Young ones

Young kea are very playful.

When they leave the nest, young kea stay close to their parents.
Their parents help them to find food and to fly.
After 4 months, young kea leave their parents to join the flock.

The older birds in a flock help feed the young ones until they are about 4 years old.

Young kea peck, claw and wrestle with each other.

Kea swing from branches, throw sticks and stones and roll around on their backs.

Danger! Beware!

Some kea are killed by falcons, stoats and rats.
Many kea die of starvation during freezing winters.
Most kea have been killed by farmers who shoot,
poison or trap them to stop them from attacking sheep.

Not many kea in the wild live longer than 15 years.

In the last 130 years, 150,000 kea have been killed to protect sheep.

Index